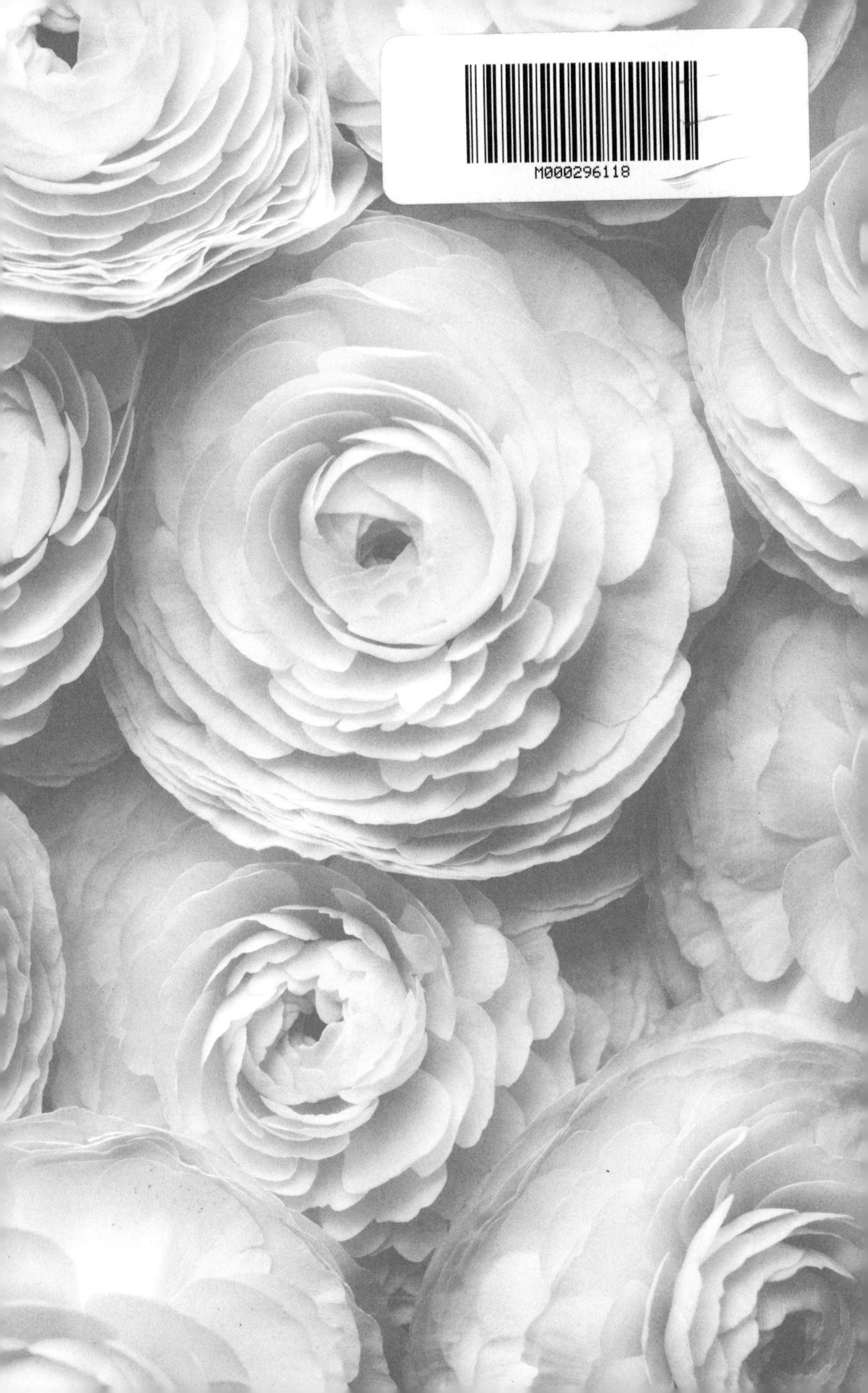

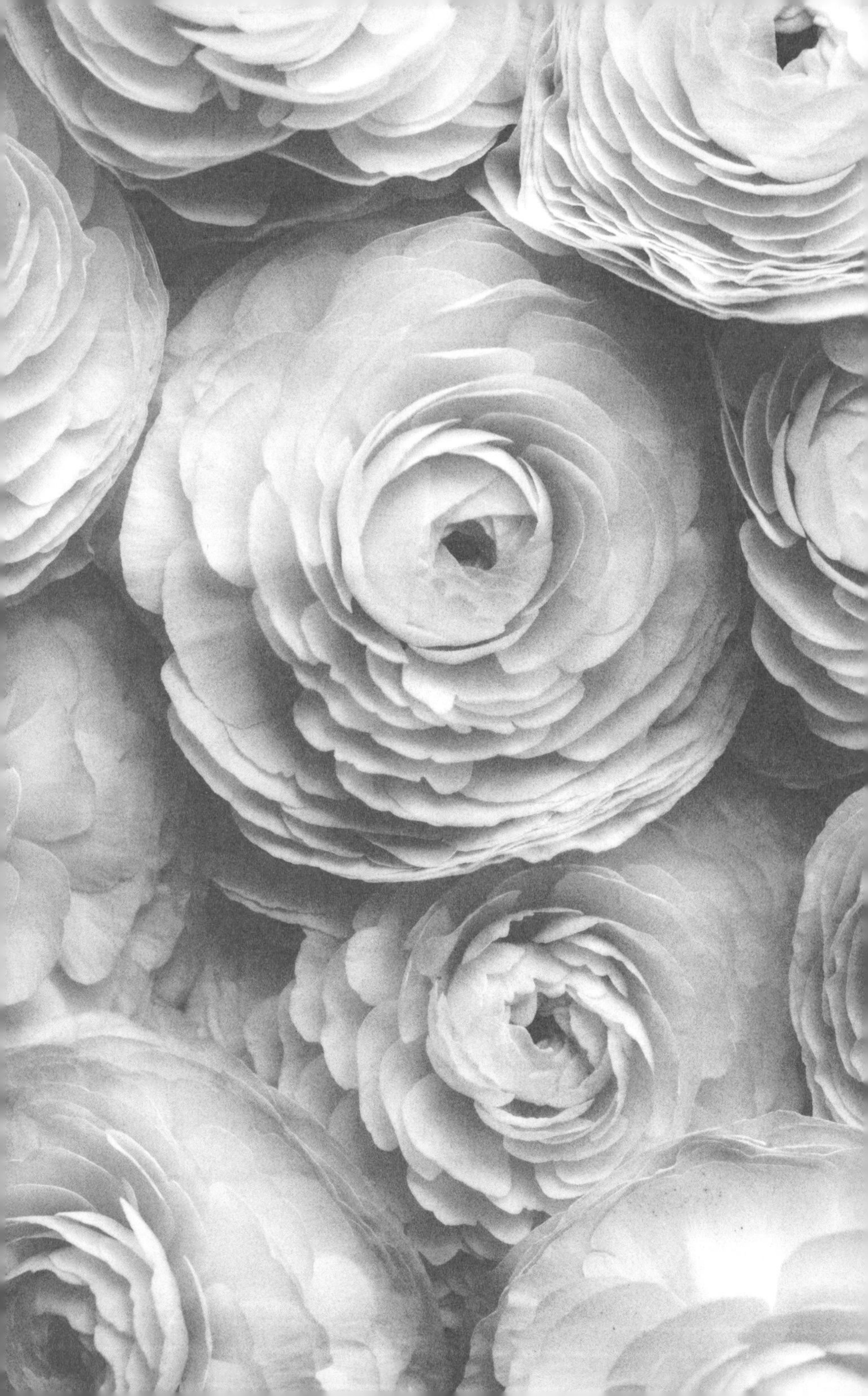

Design by Hana Anouk Nakamura
Calligraphy by Nim Ben-Reuven

ISBN 978-1-4197-2717-7

Printed and bound in China
10 9 8 7 6 5 4 3 2 1

ABRAMS The Art of Books
abramsbooks.com

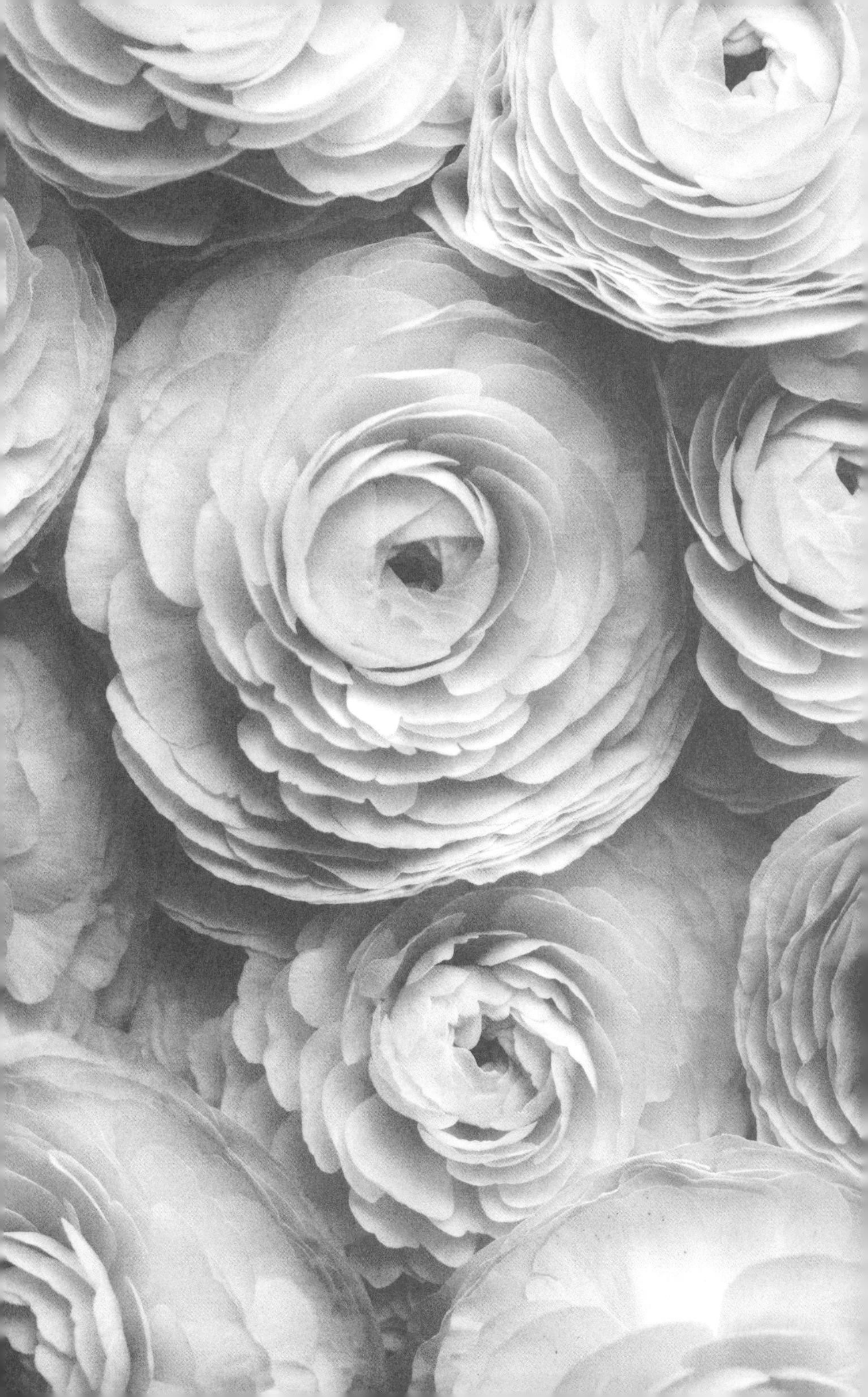

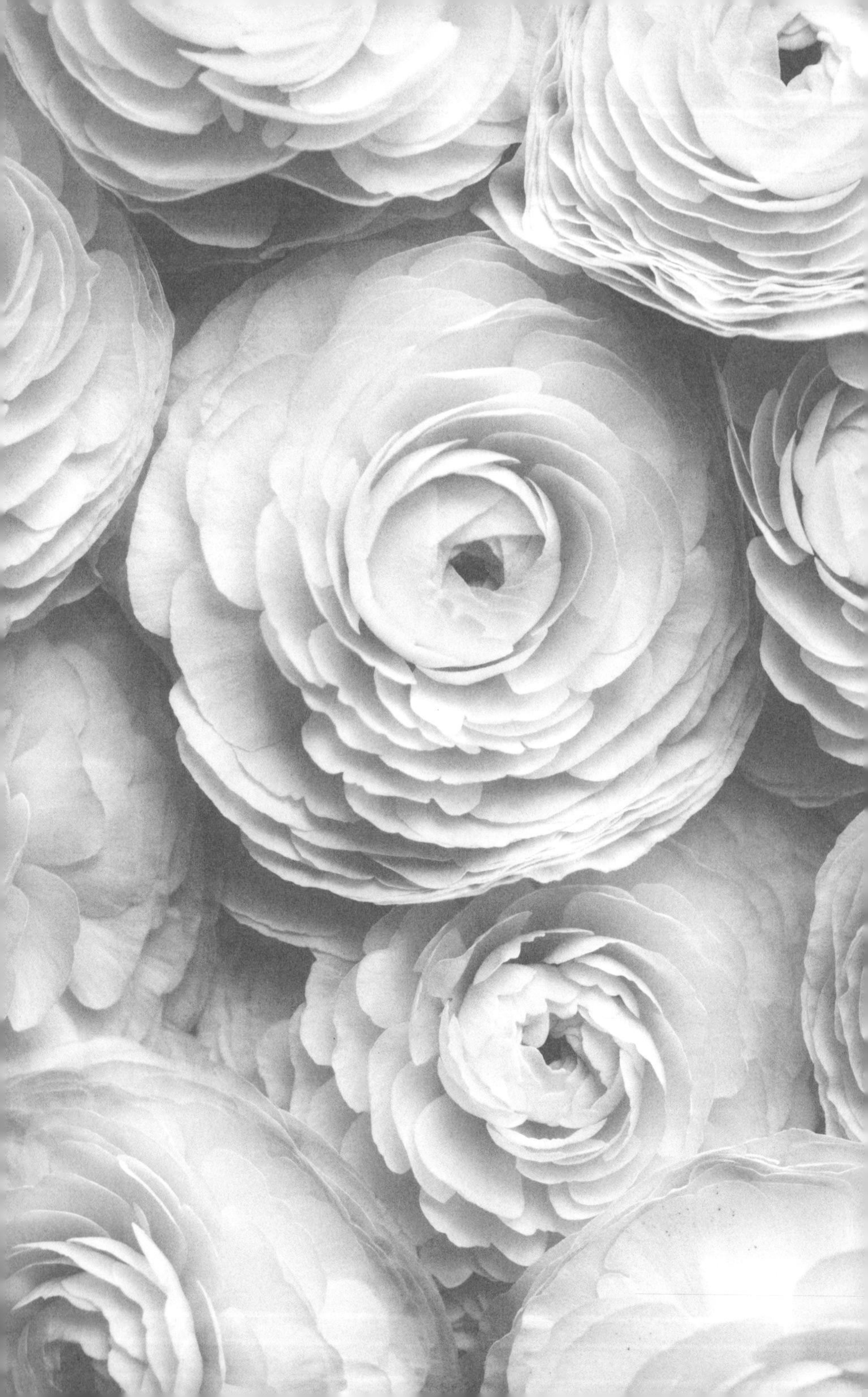